Erotic Art Techniques For Mature Artists

How To Properly Draw Erotic Subjects

Erotic

By : Adult Arts

Published By:

Adult Arts

ISBN-13: **978-1522708438**
ISBN-10: **152270843X**

©Copyright 2015 – Adult Arts

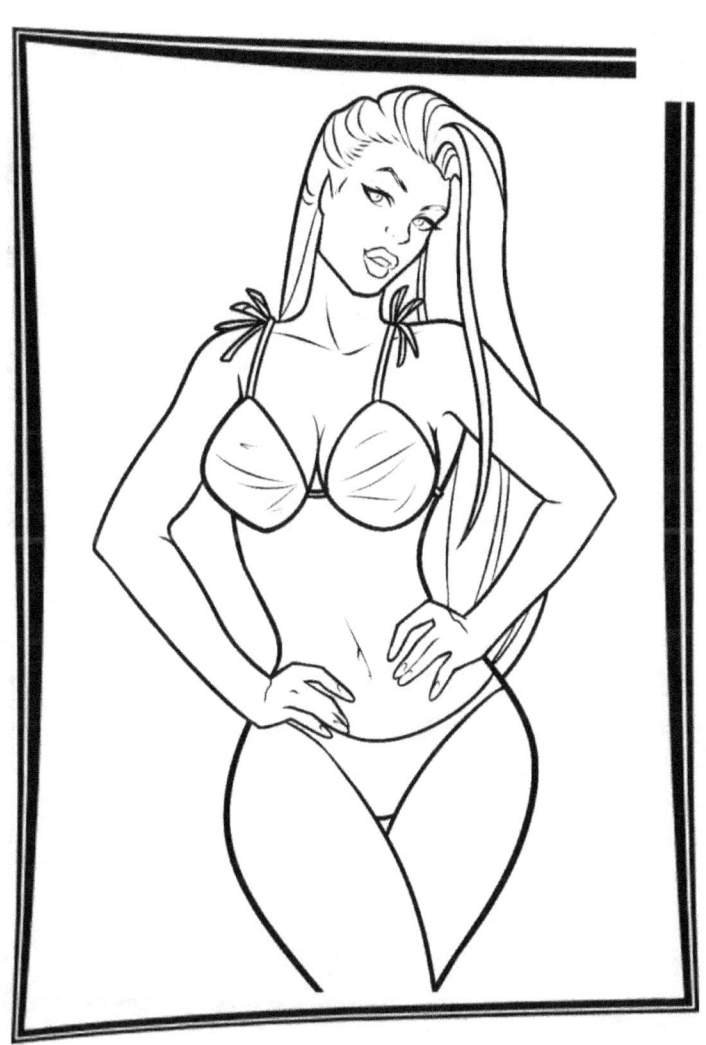

ART 1

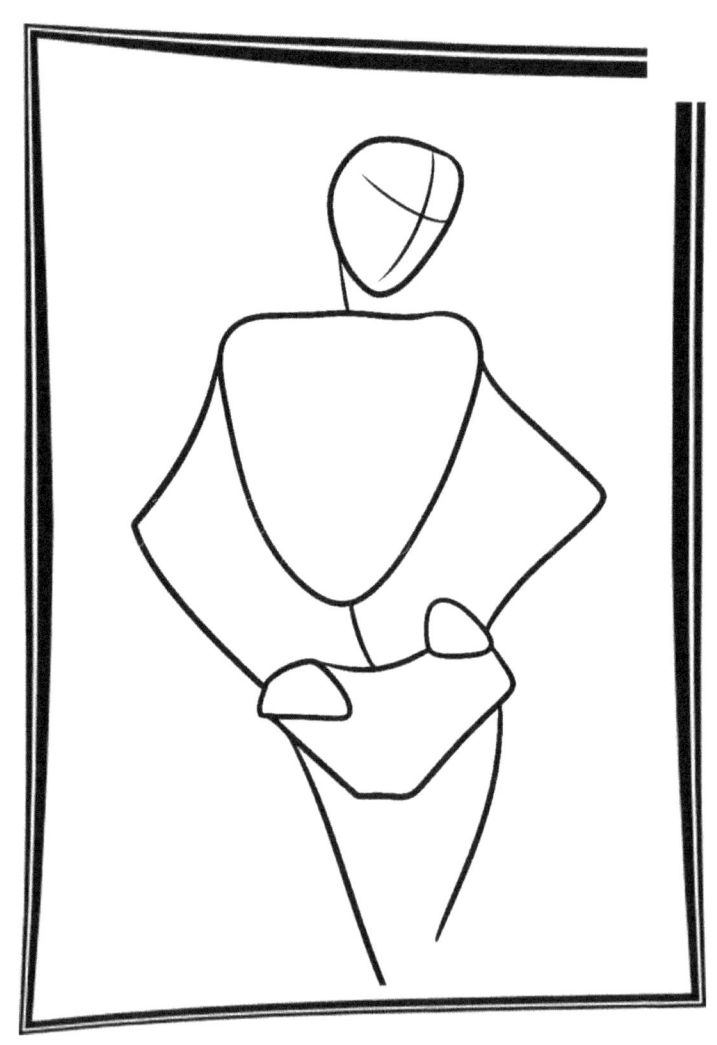

STEP 1

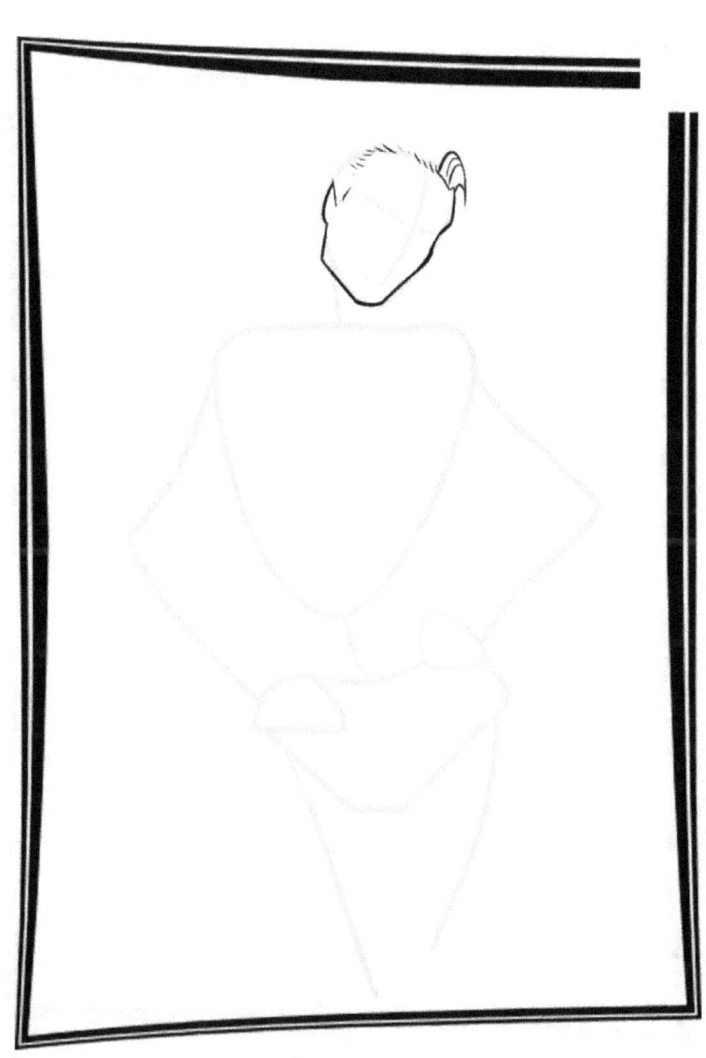

STEP 2

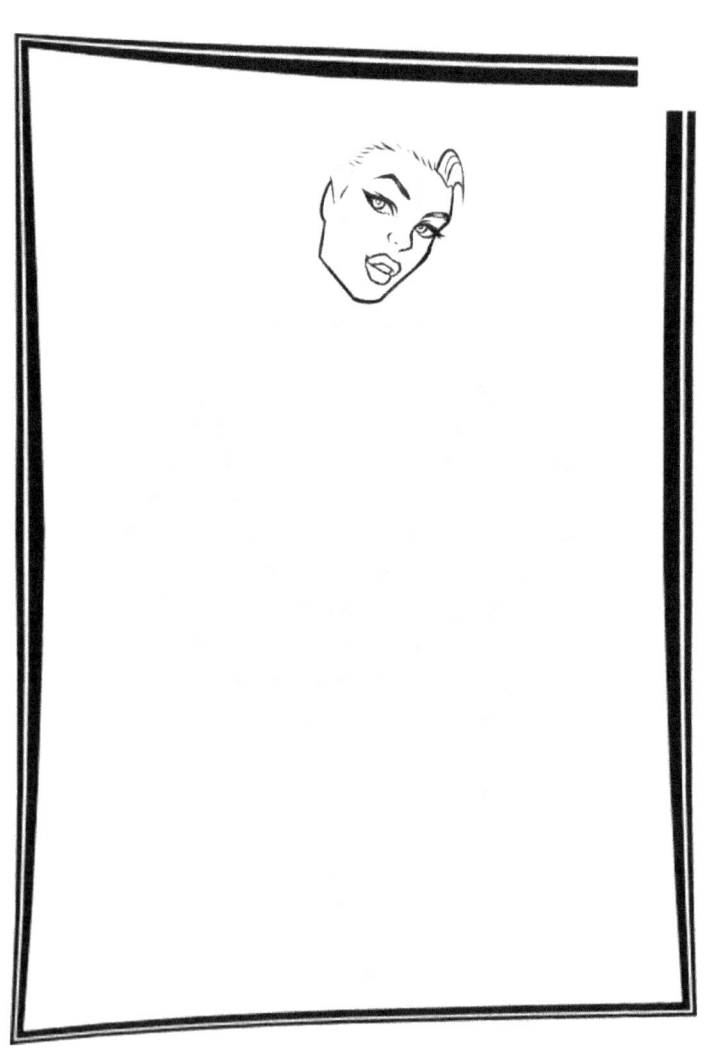

STEP 3

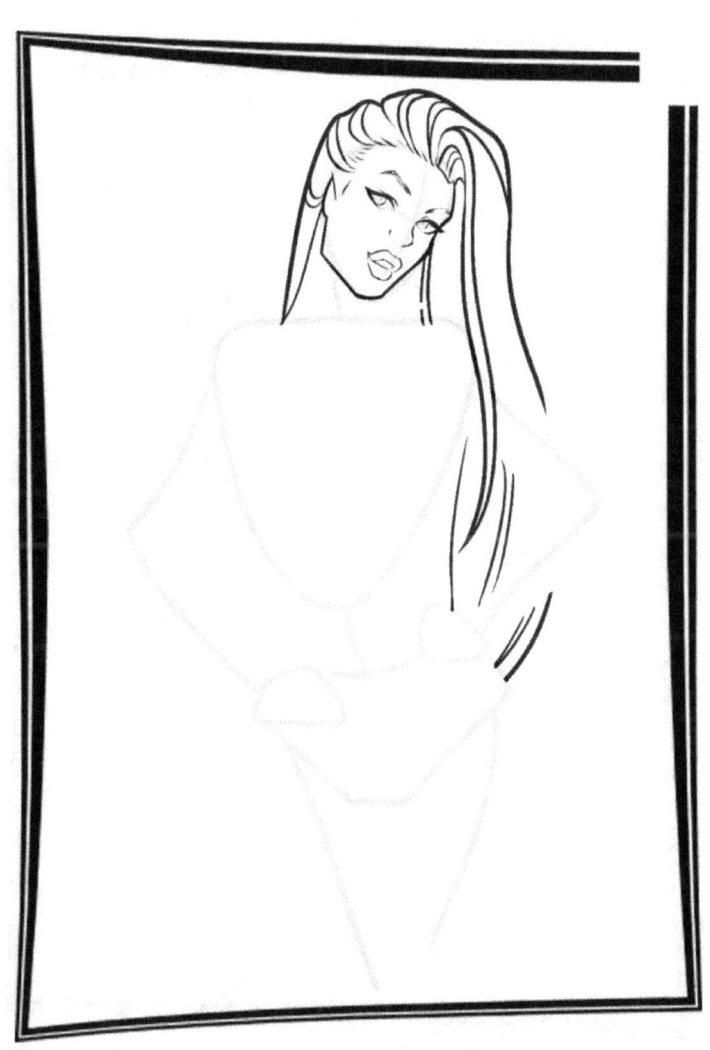

STEP 4

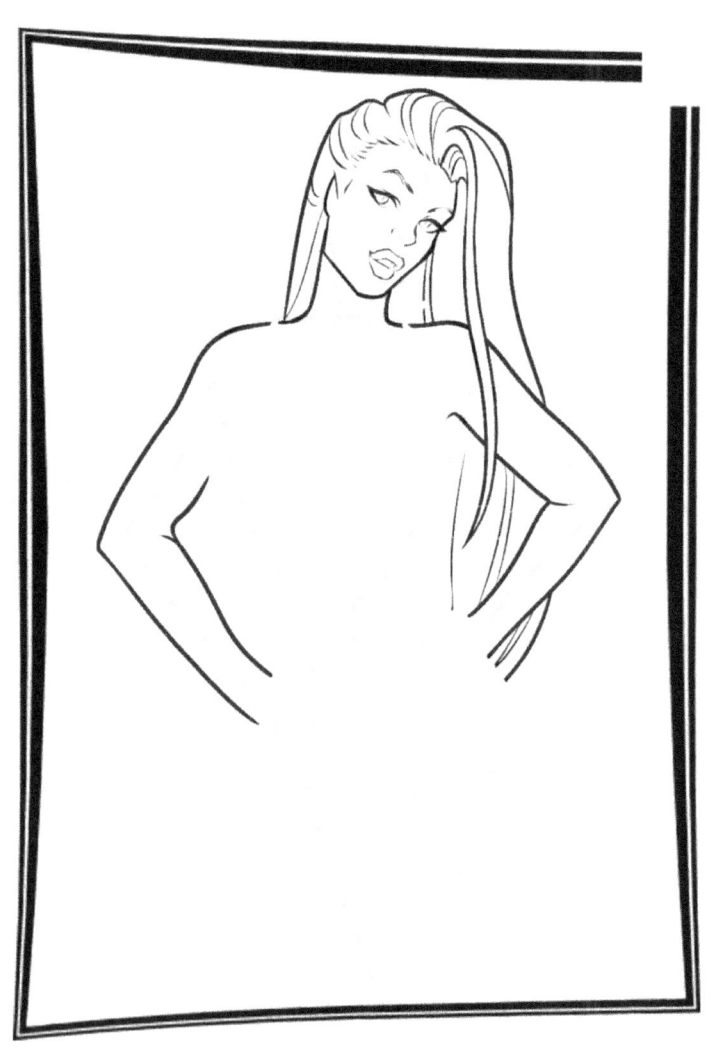

STEP 5

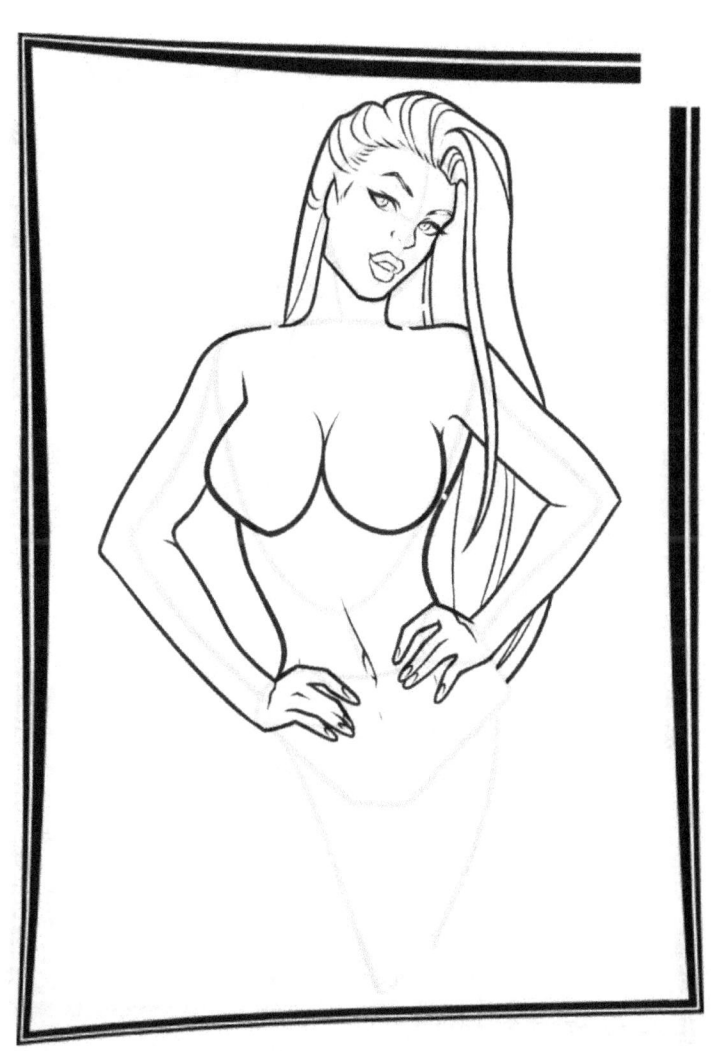

STEP 6

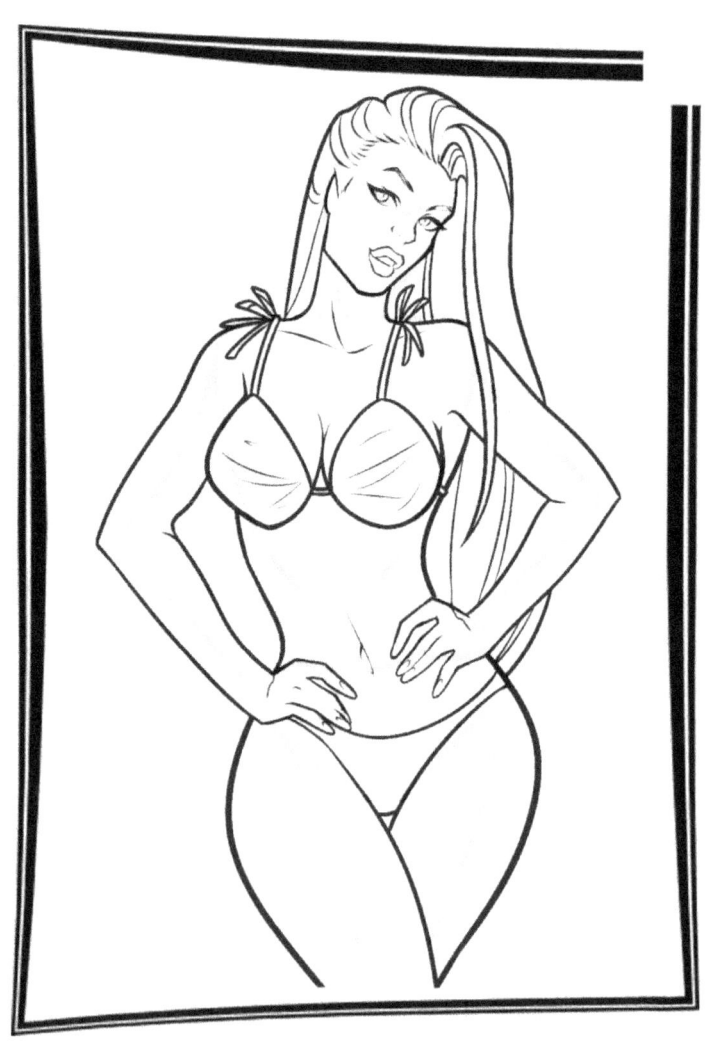

STEP 7

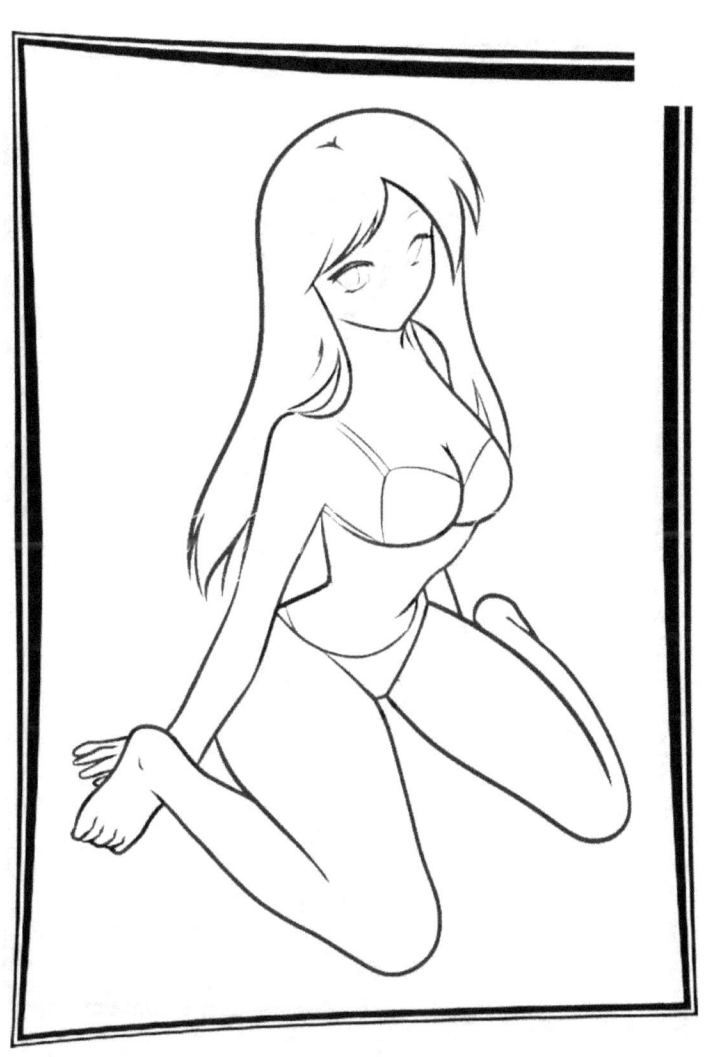

ART 2

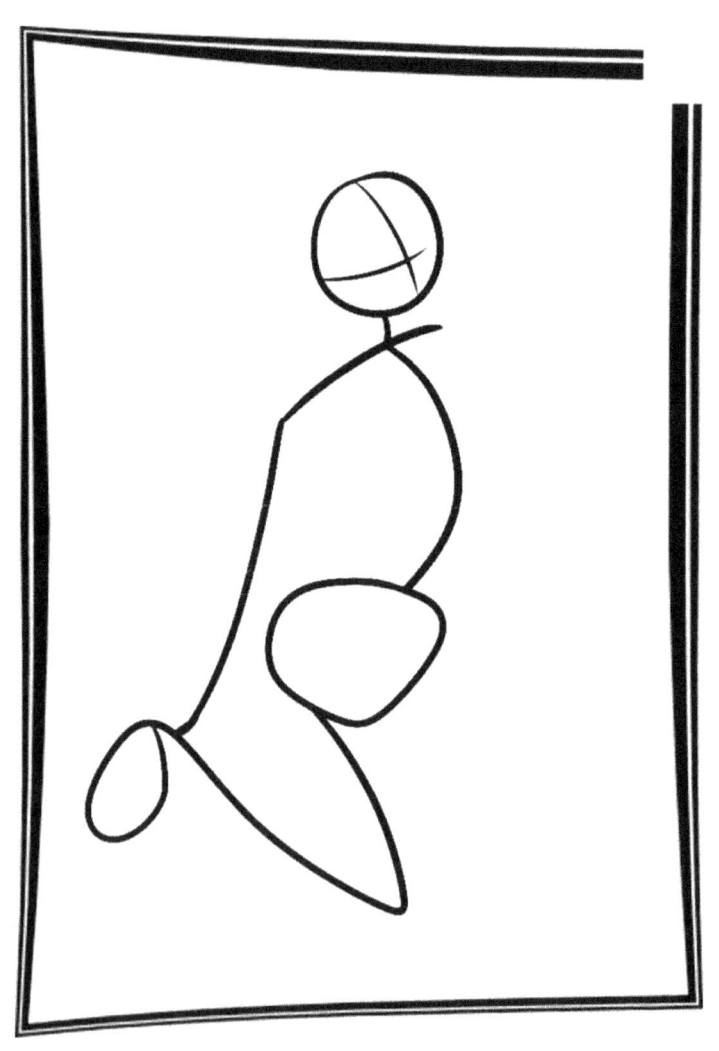

STEP 1

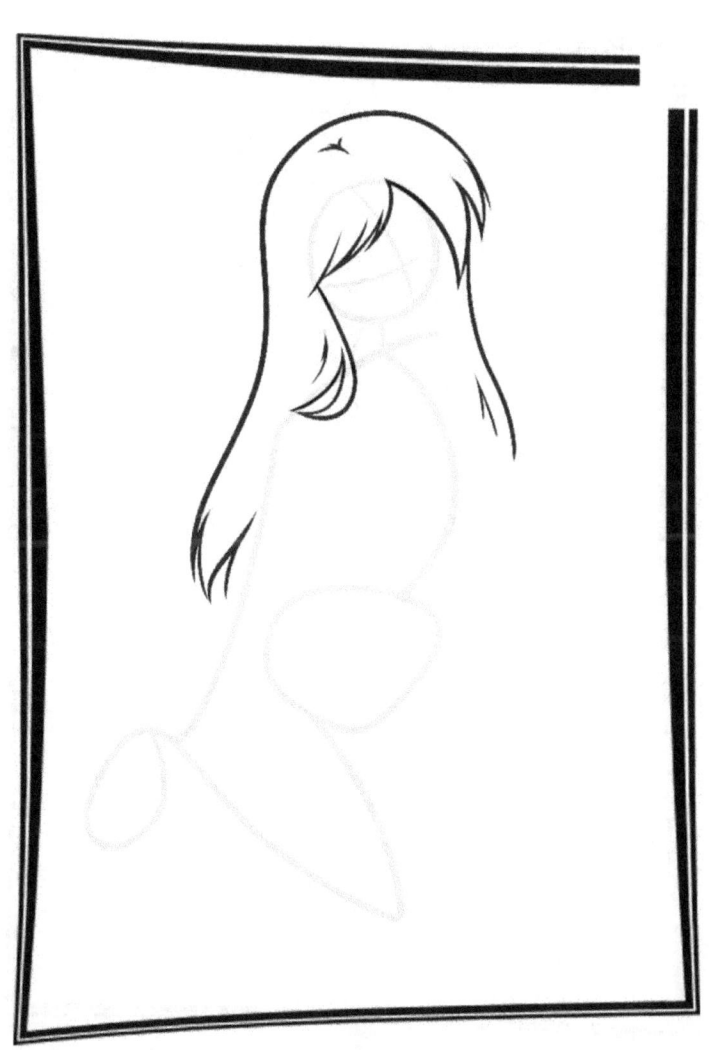

STEP 2

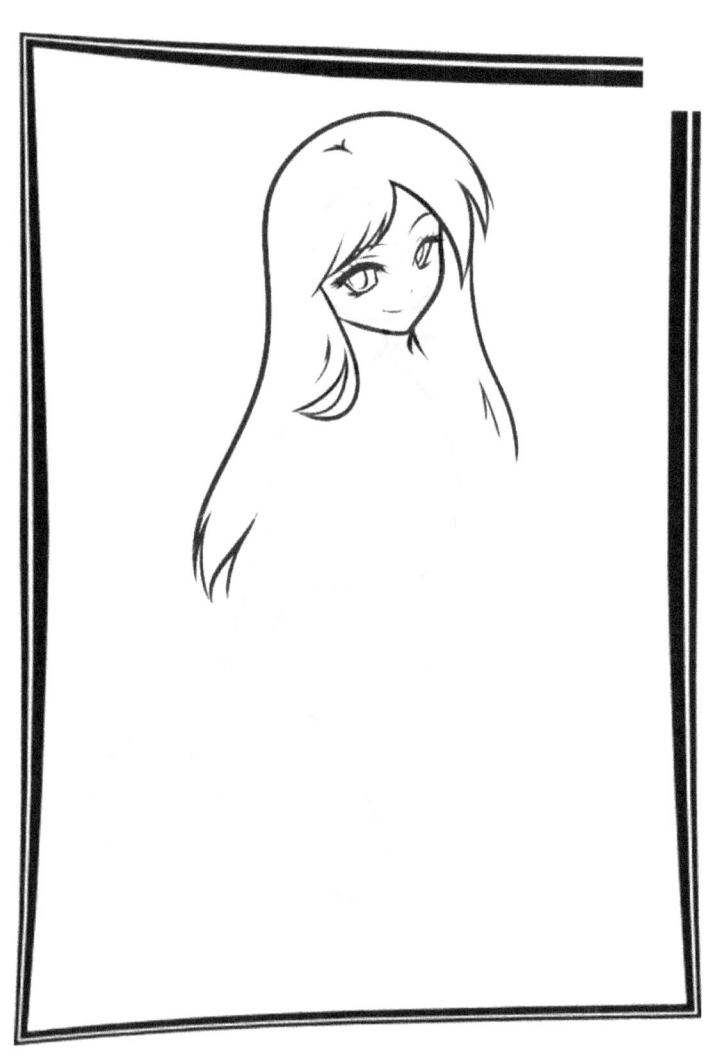

STEP 3

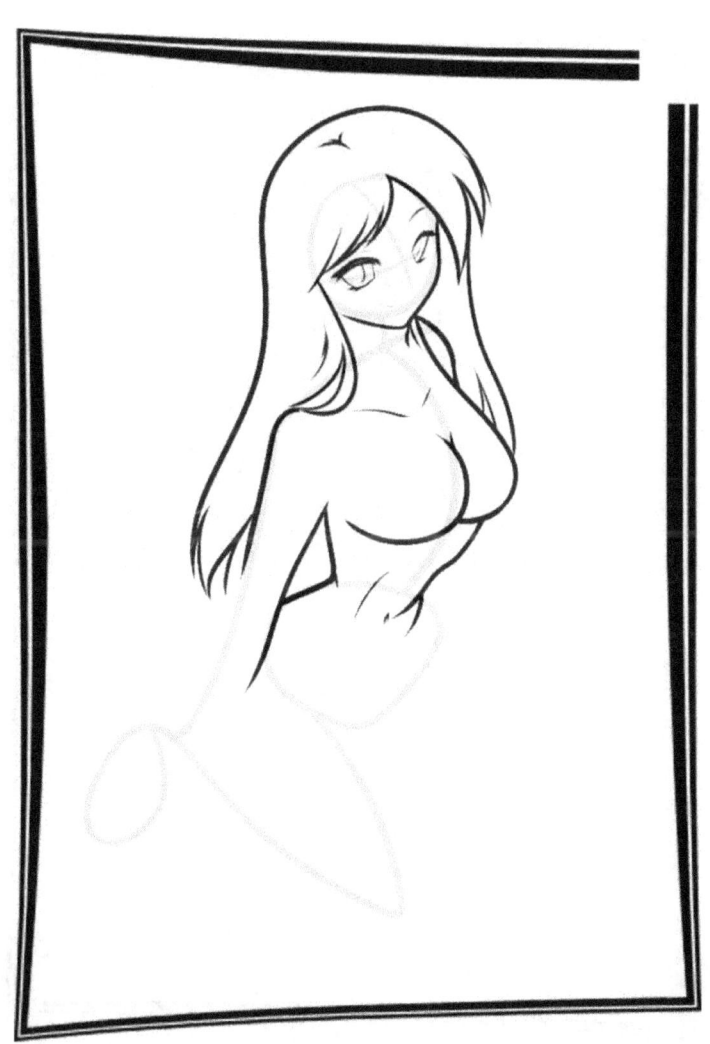

STEP 4

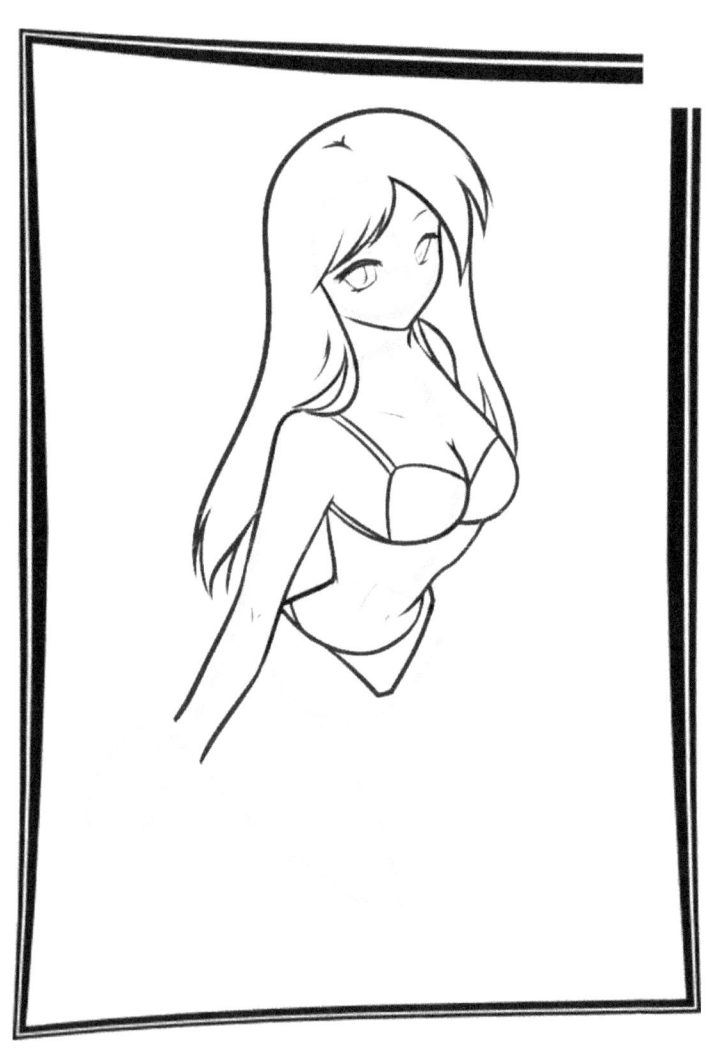

STEP 5

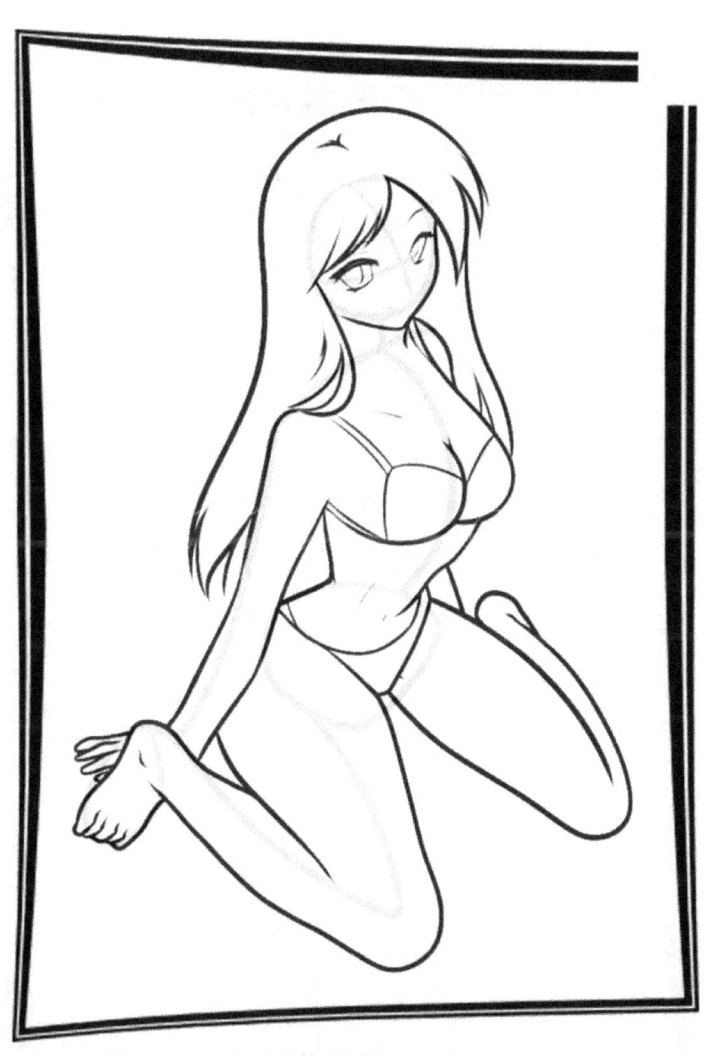

STEP 6

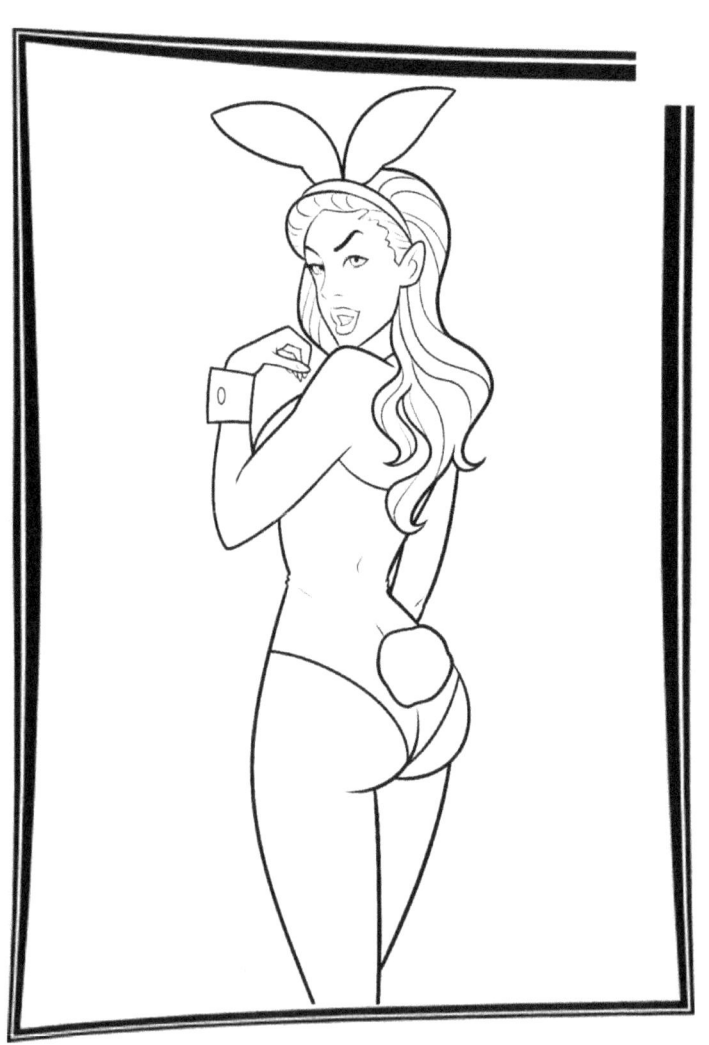

ART 3

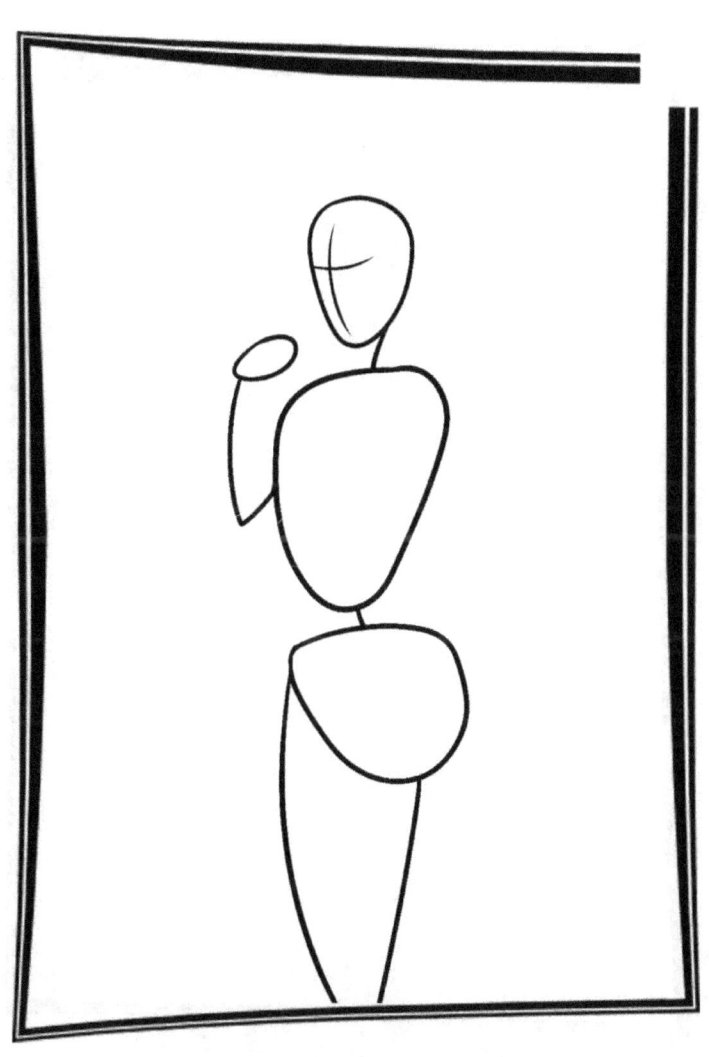

STEP 1

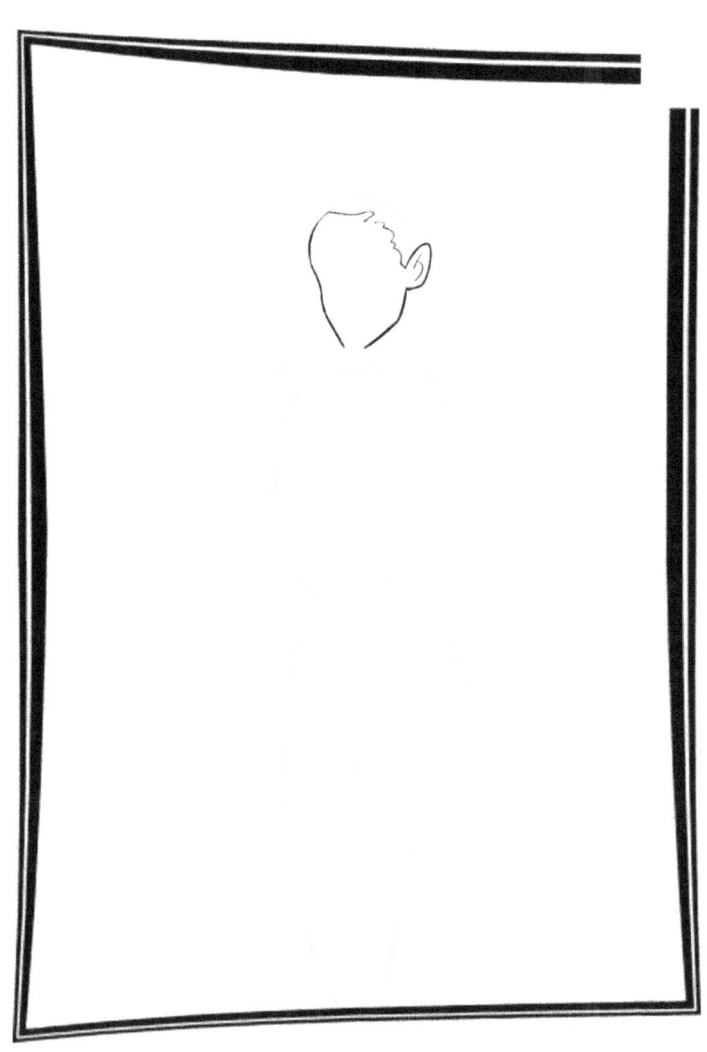

STEP 2

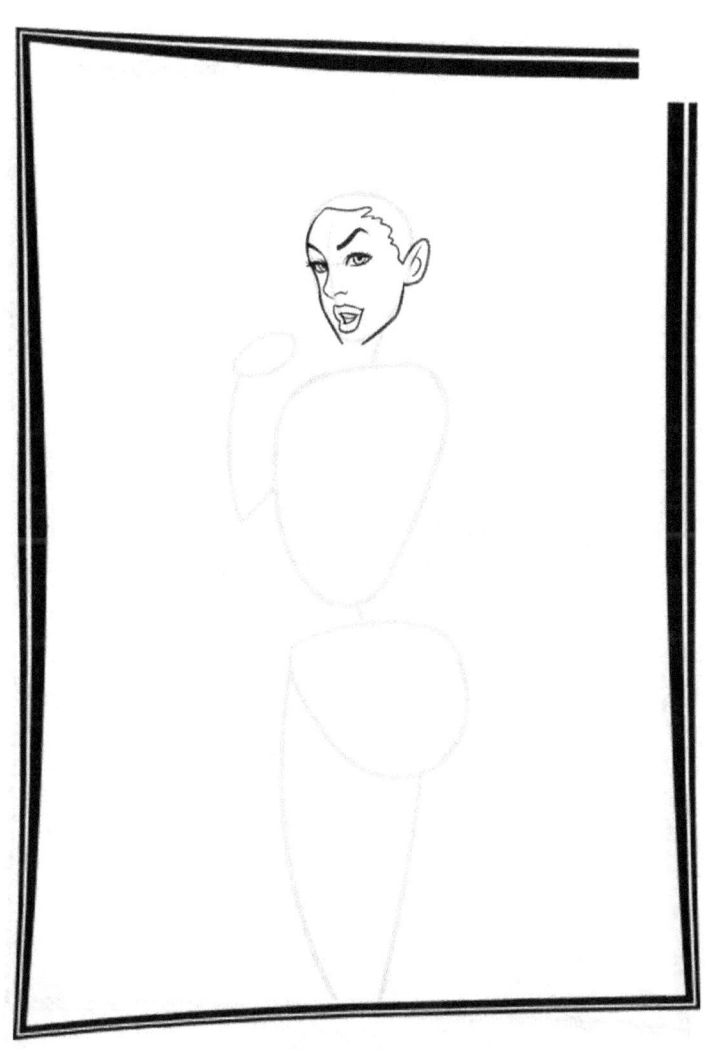

STEP 3

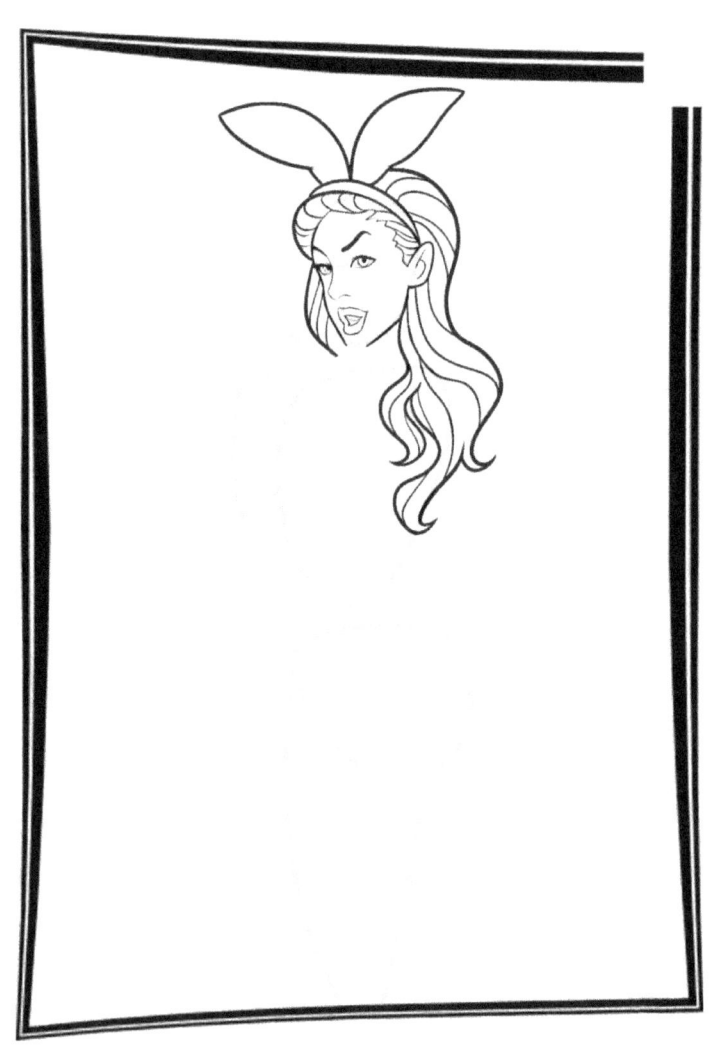

STEP 4

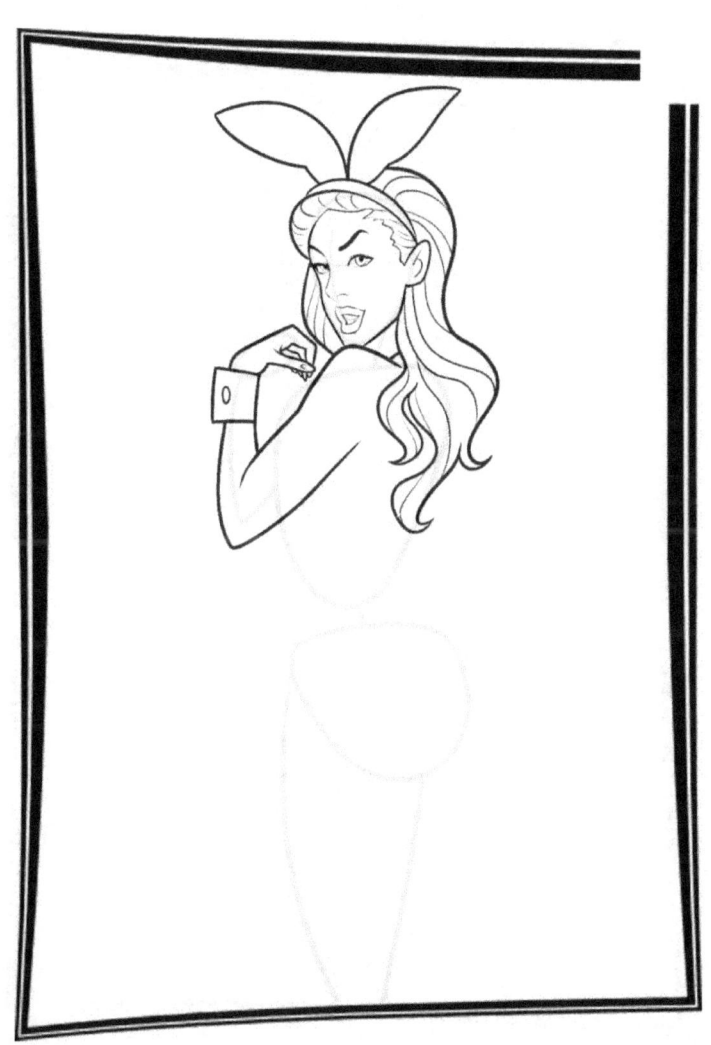

STEP 5

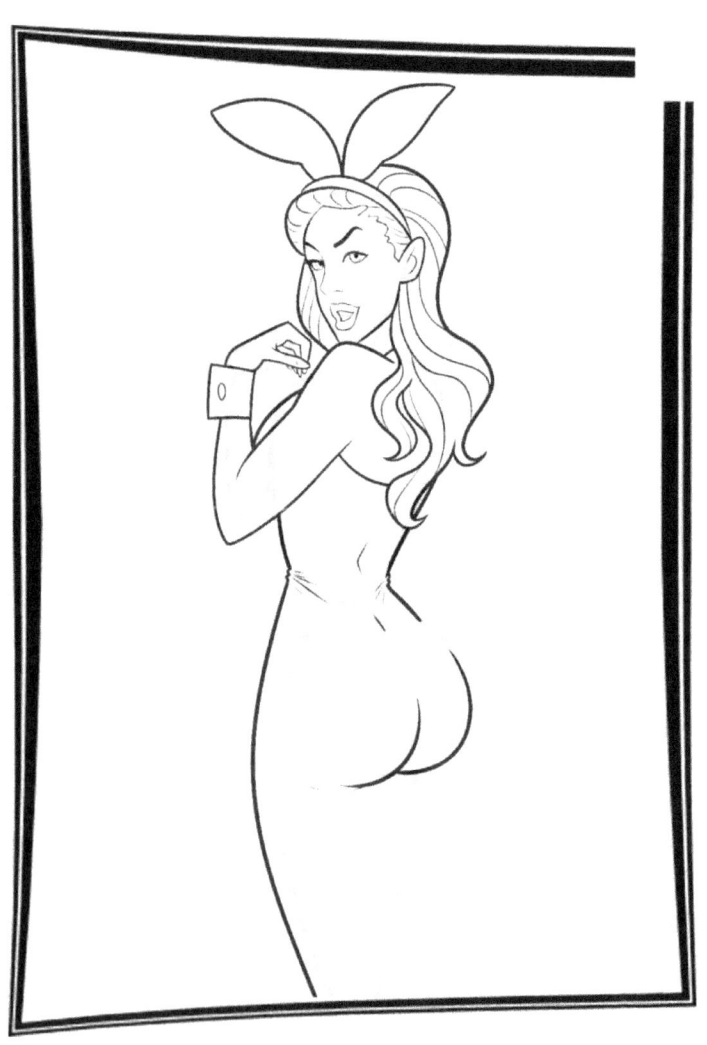

STEP 6

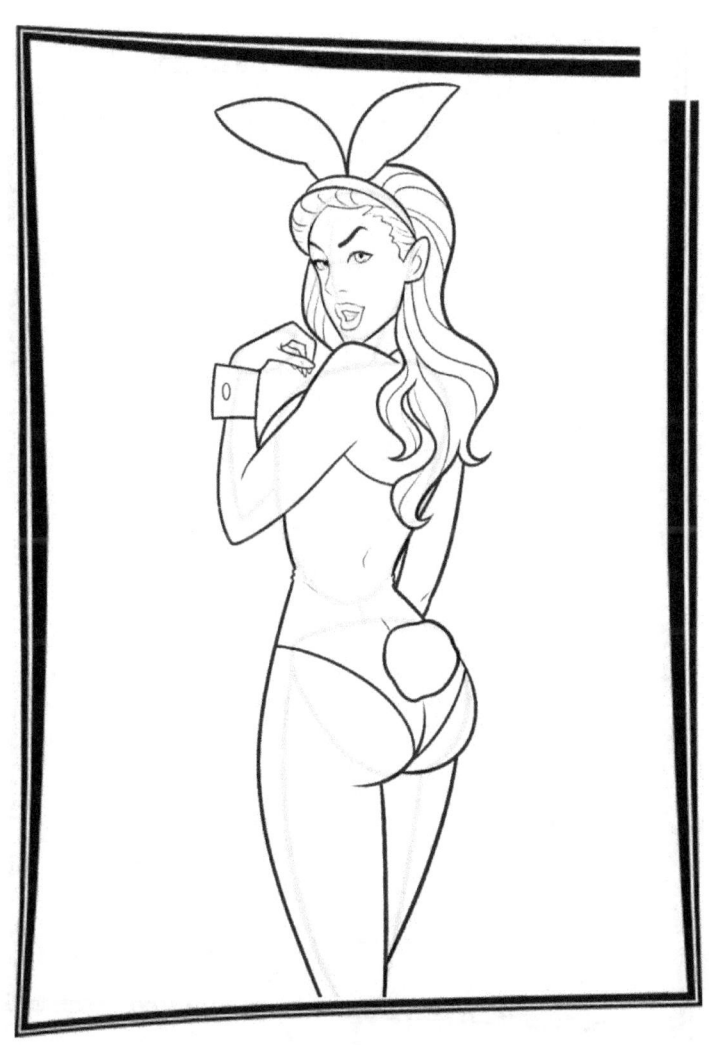

STEP 7

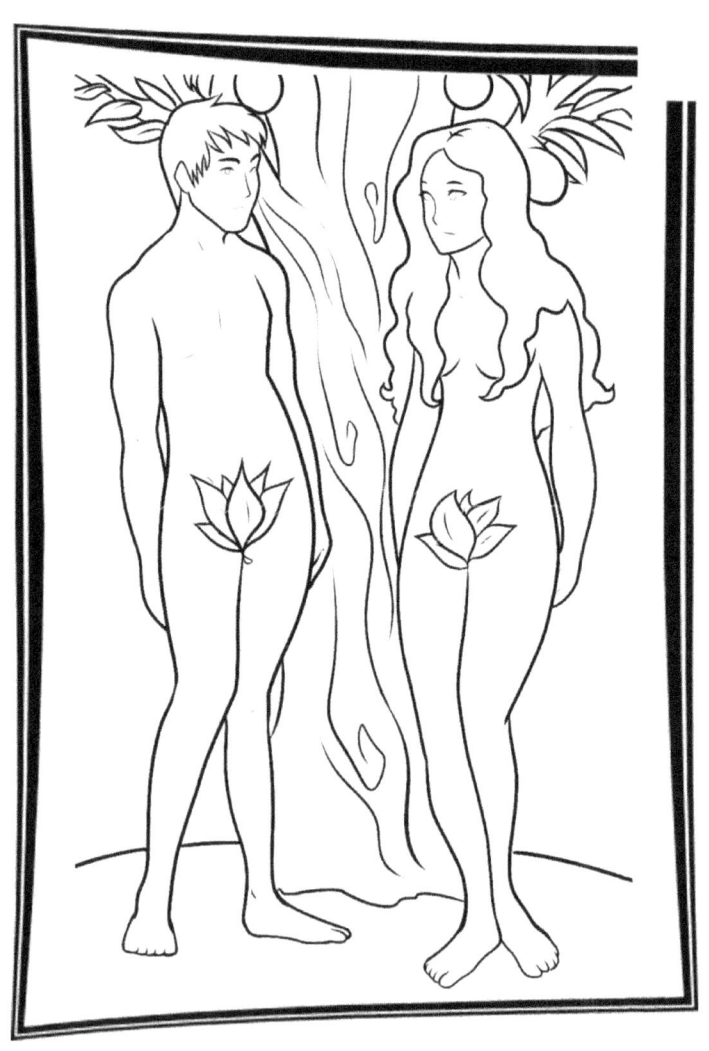

ART 4

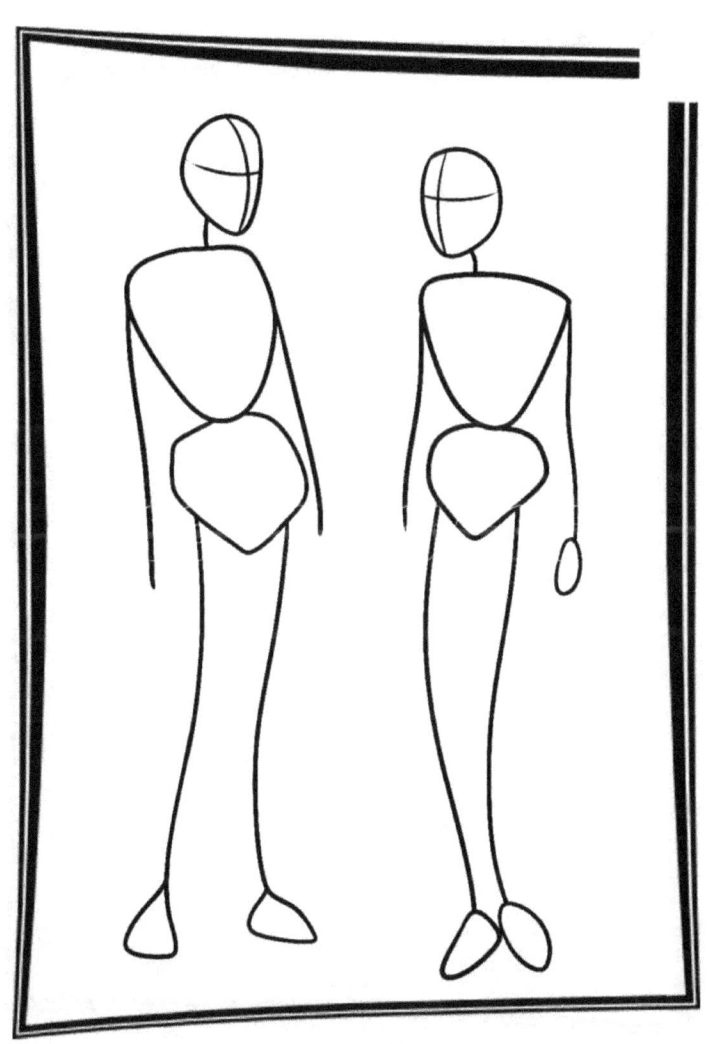

STEP 1

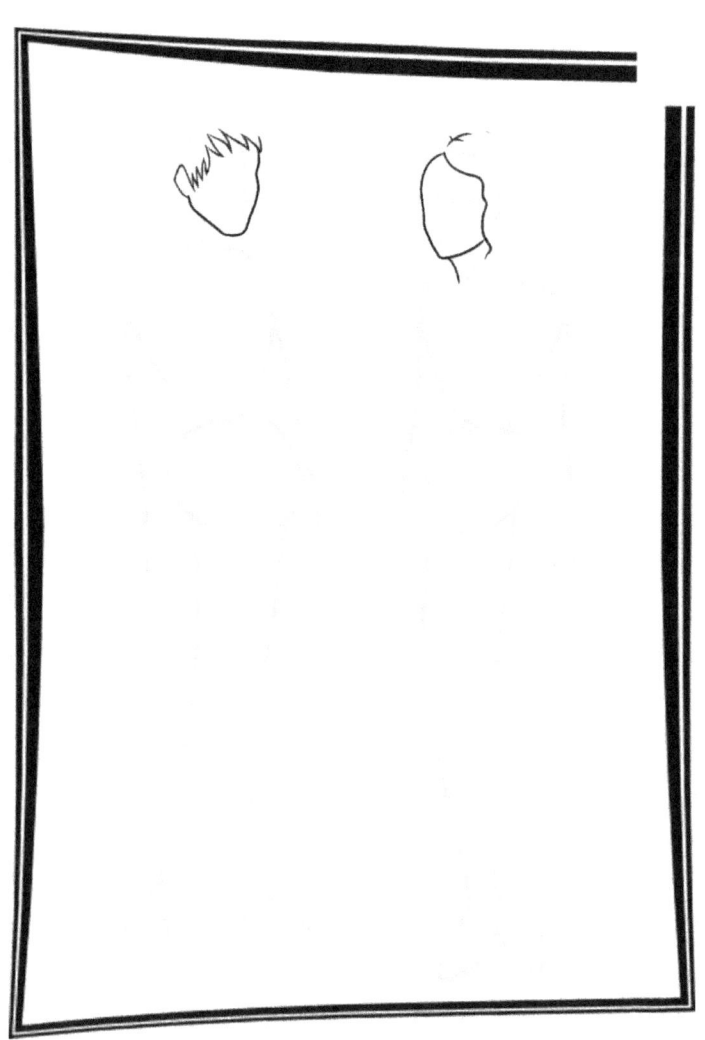

STEP 2

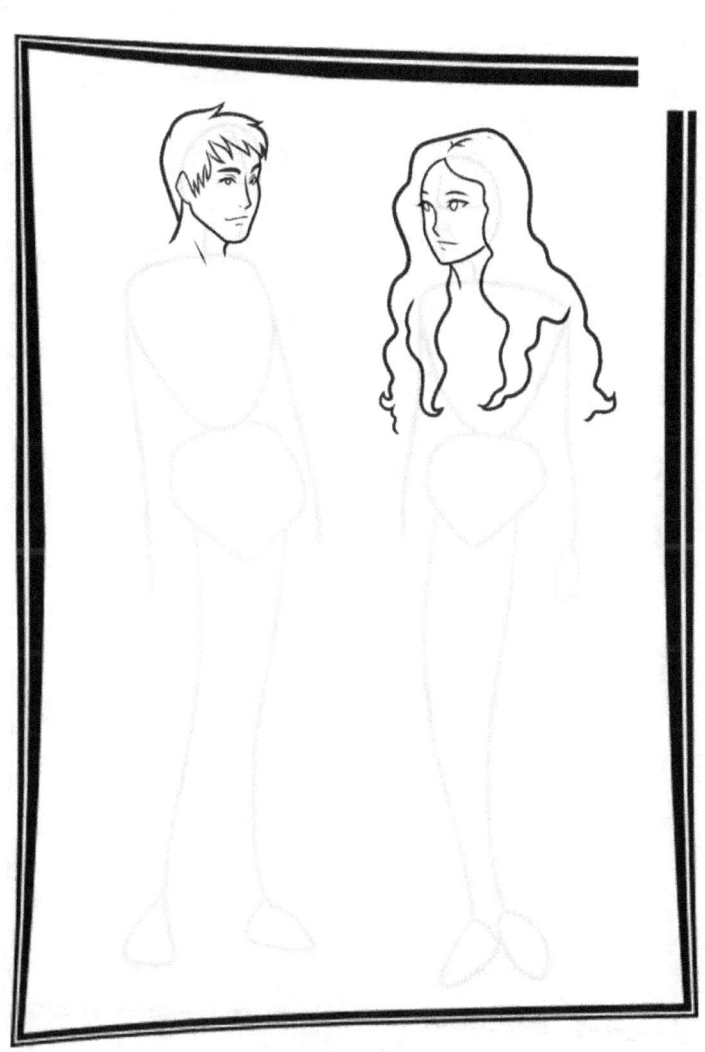

STEP 3

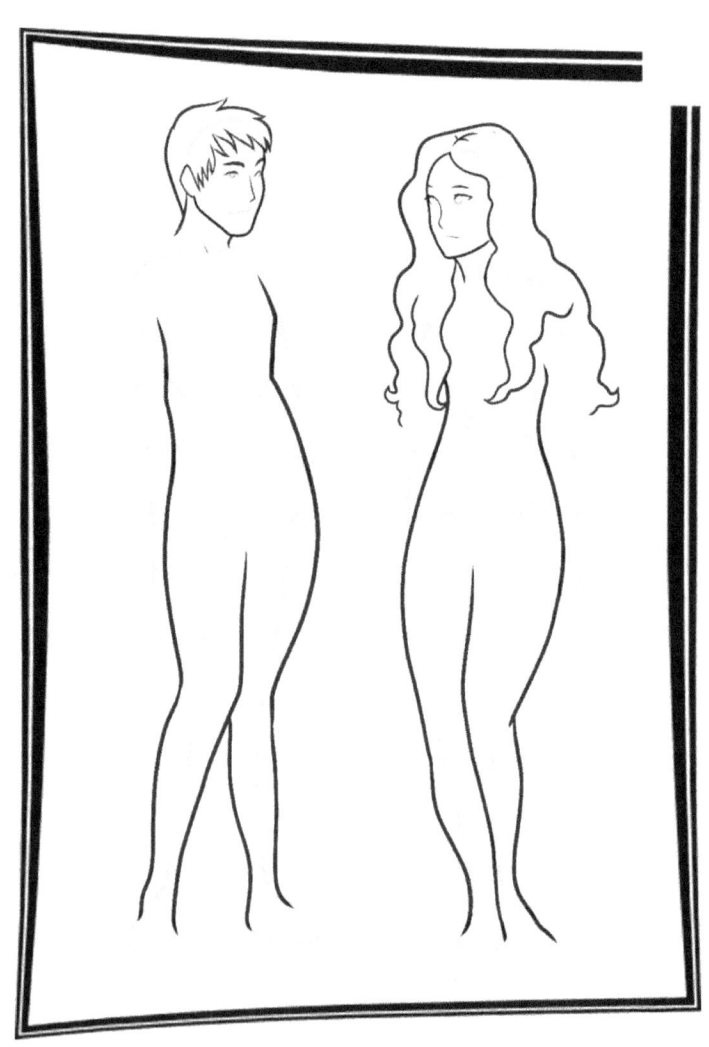

STEP 4

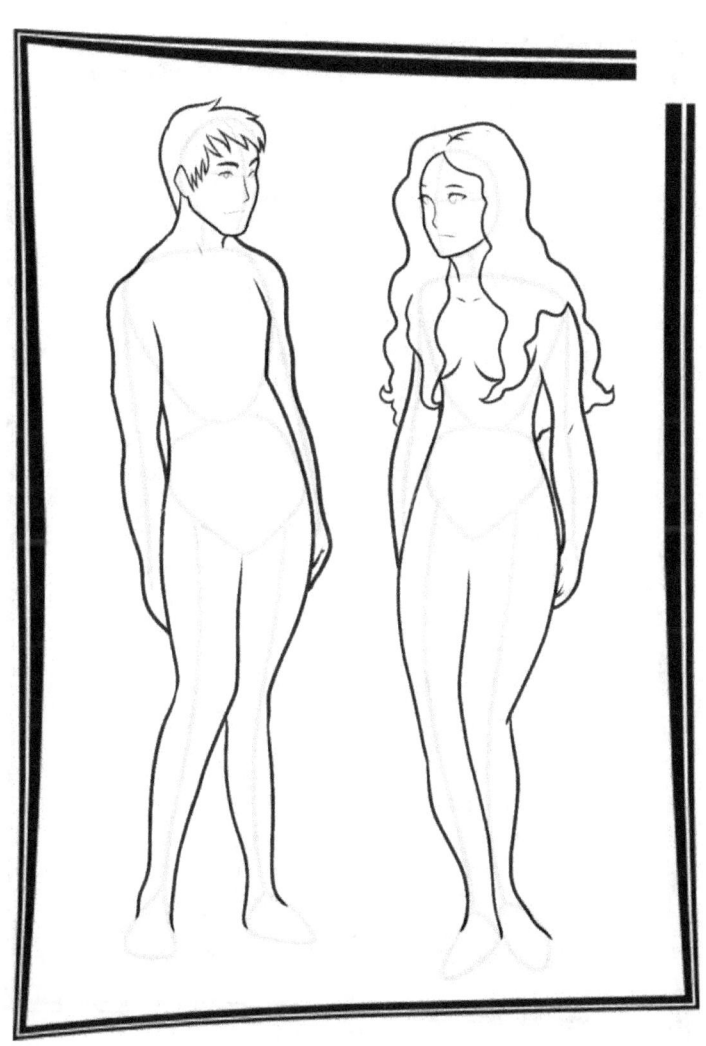

STEP 5

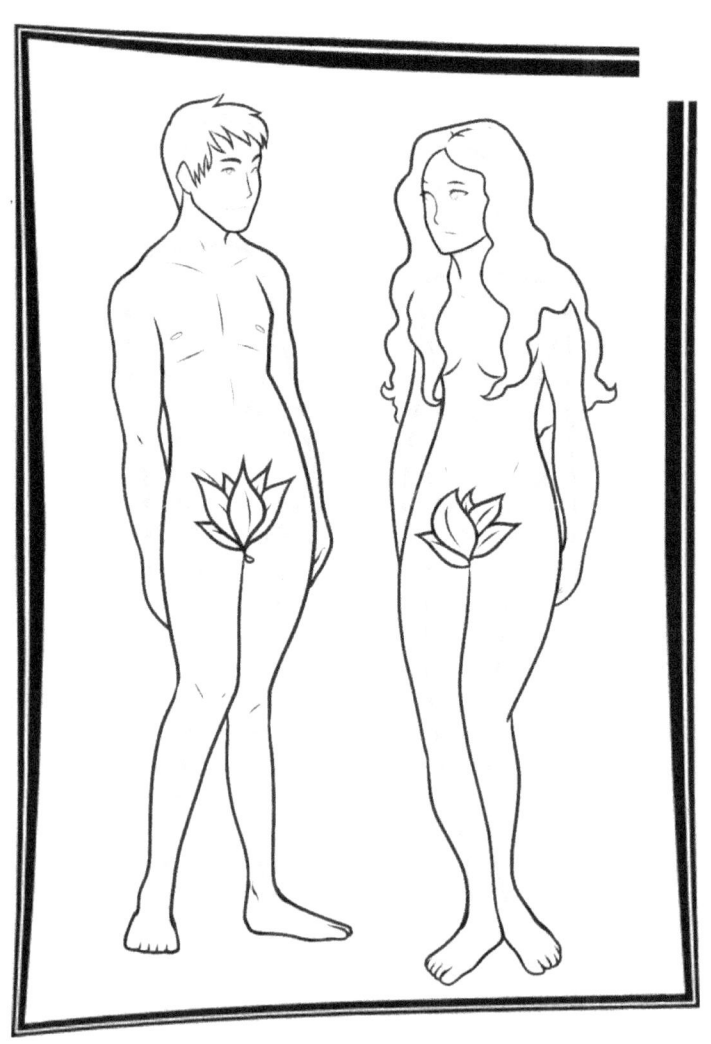

STEP 6

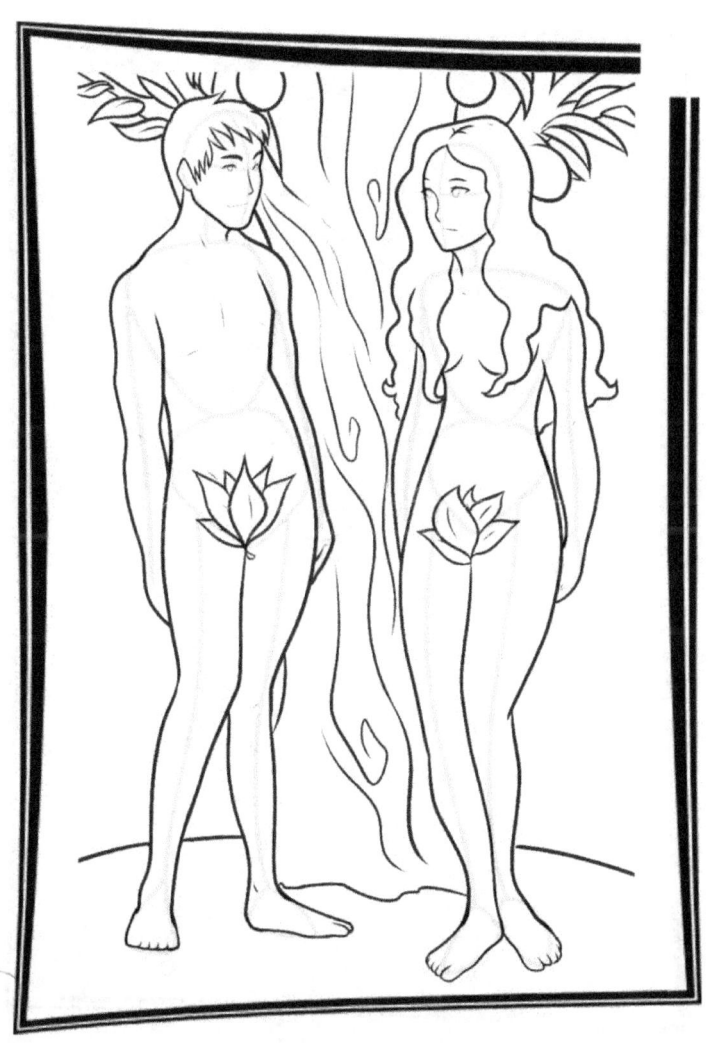

STEP 7

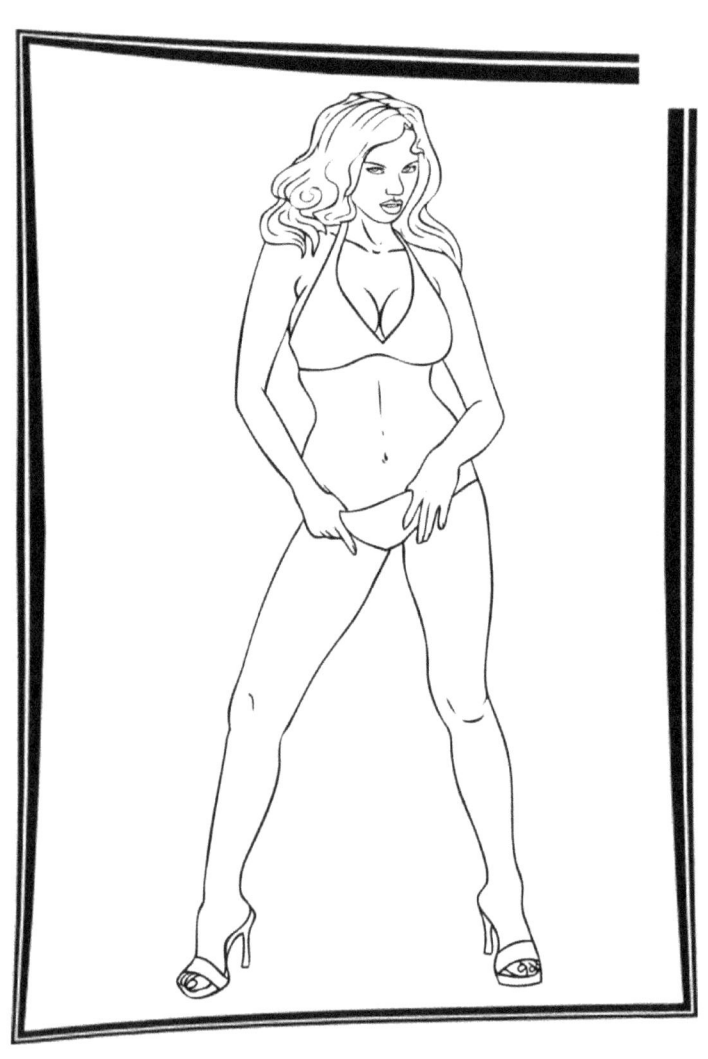

ART 5

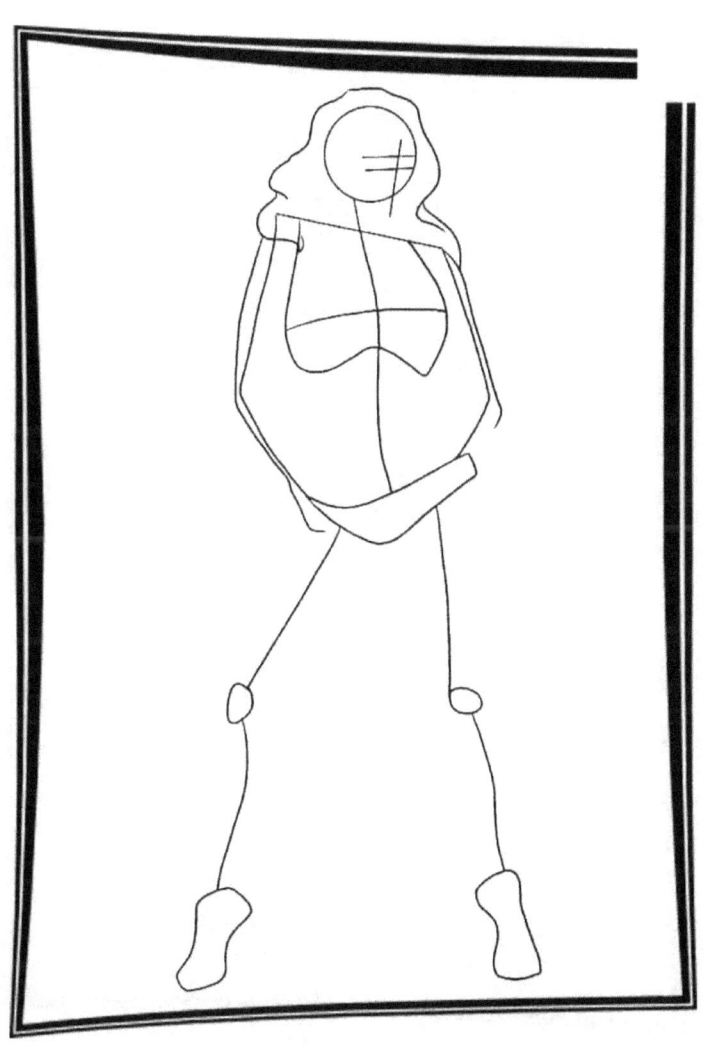

STEP 1

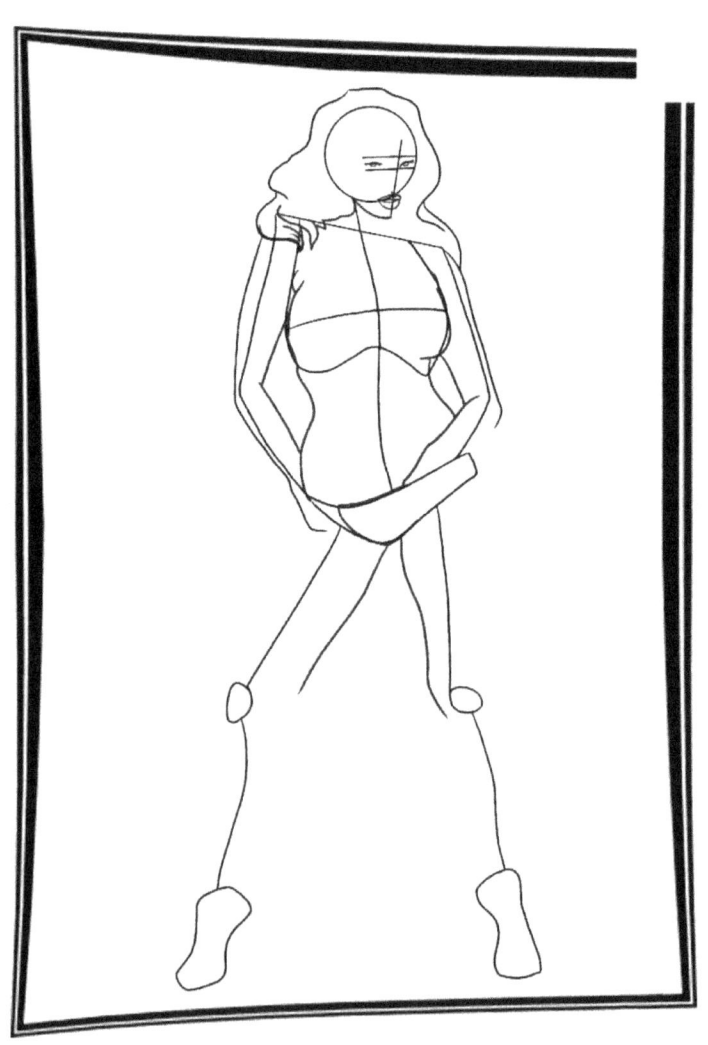

STEP 2

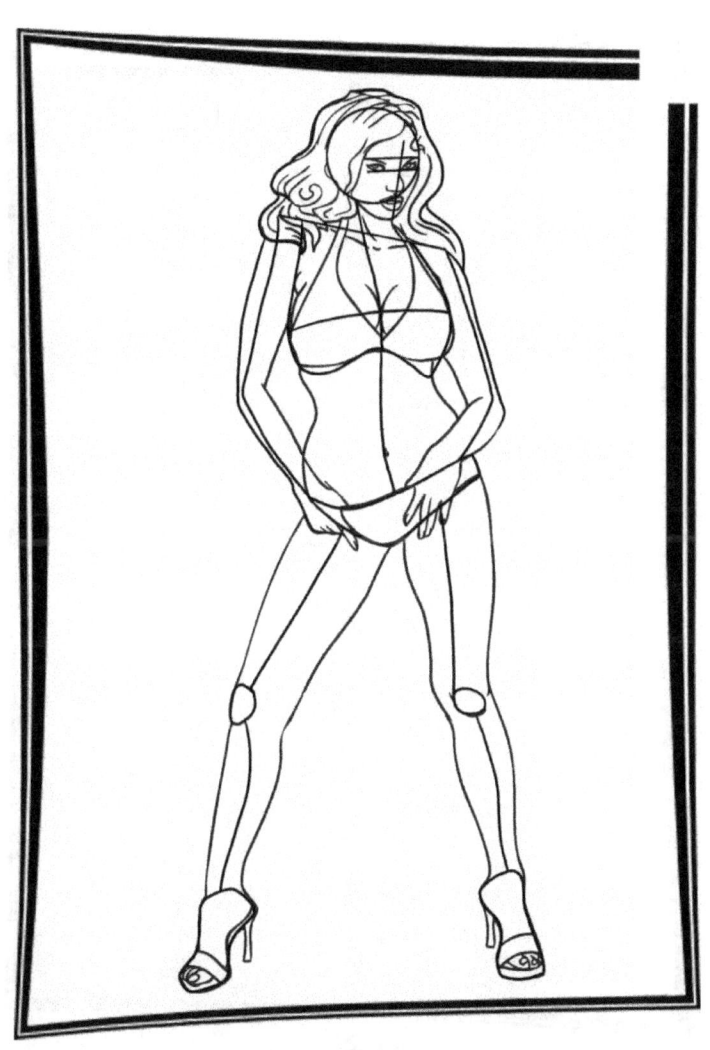

STEP 3

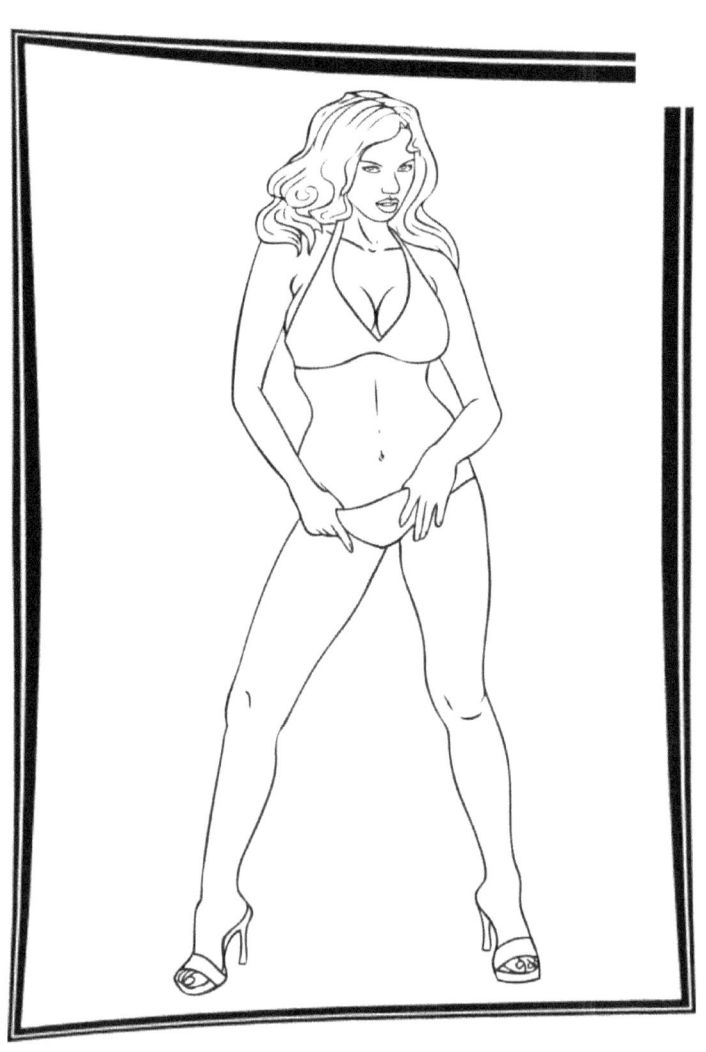

STEP 4

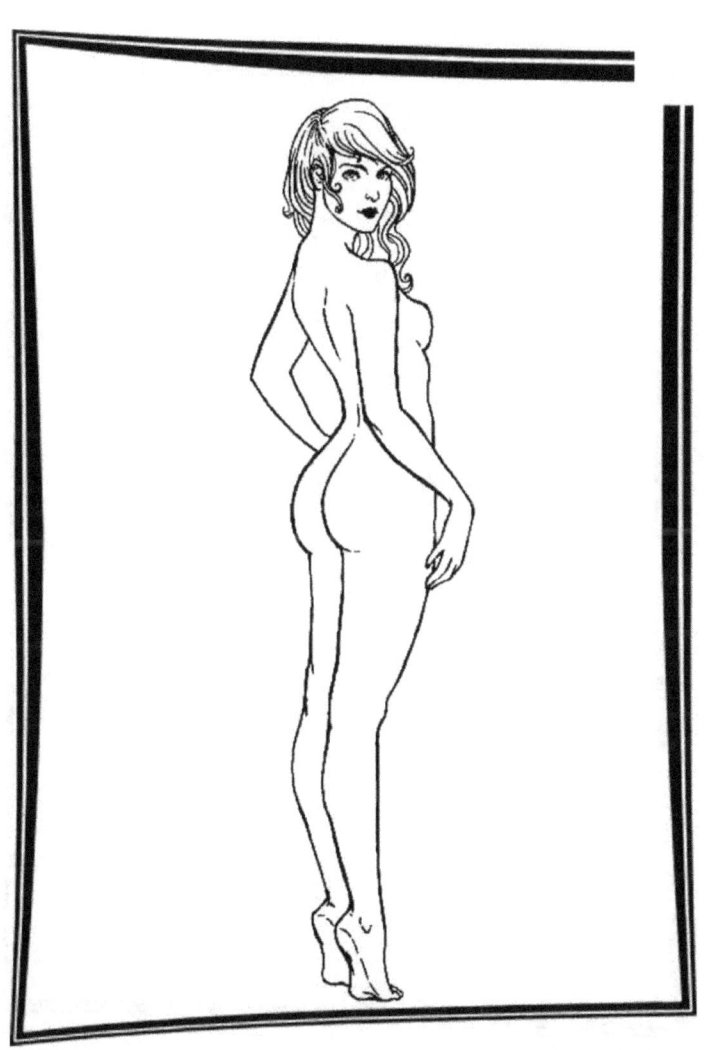

ART 6

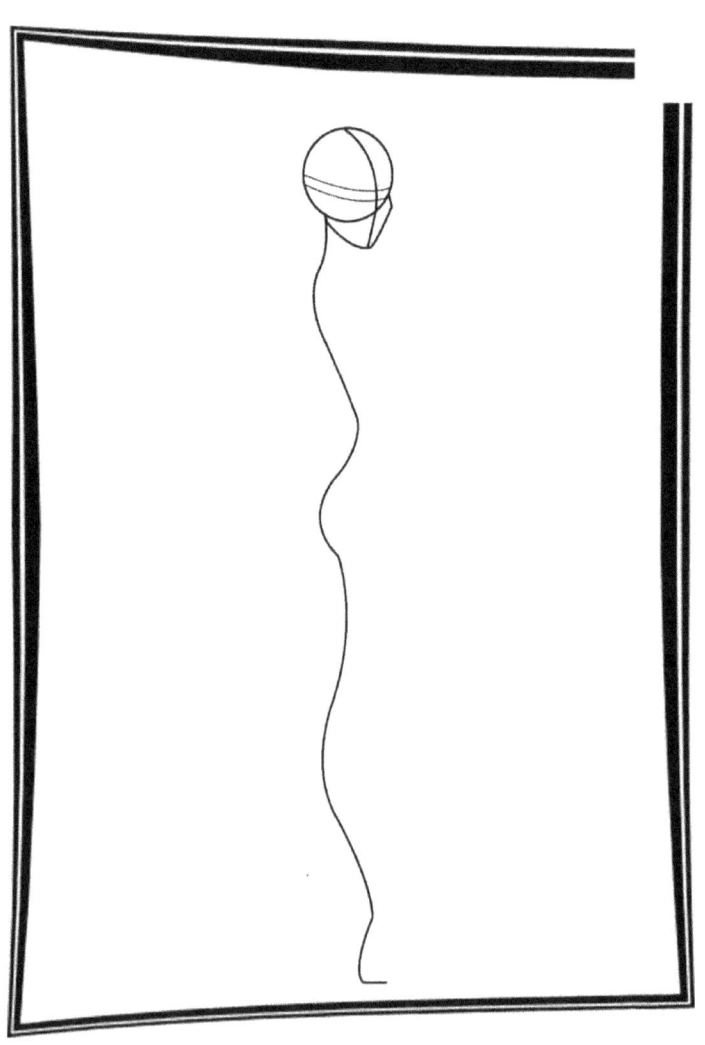

STEP 1

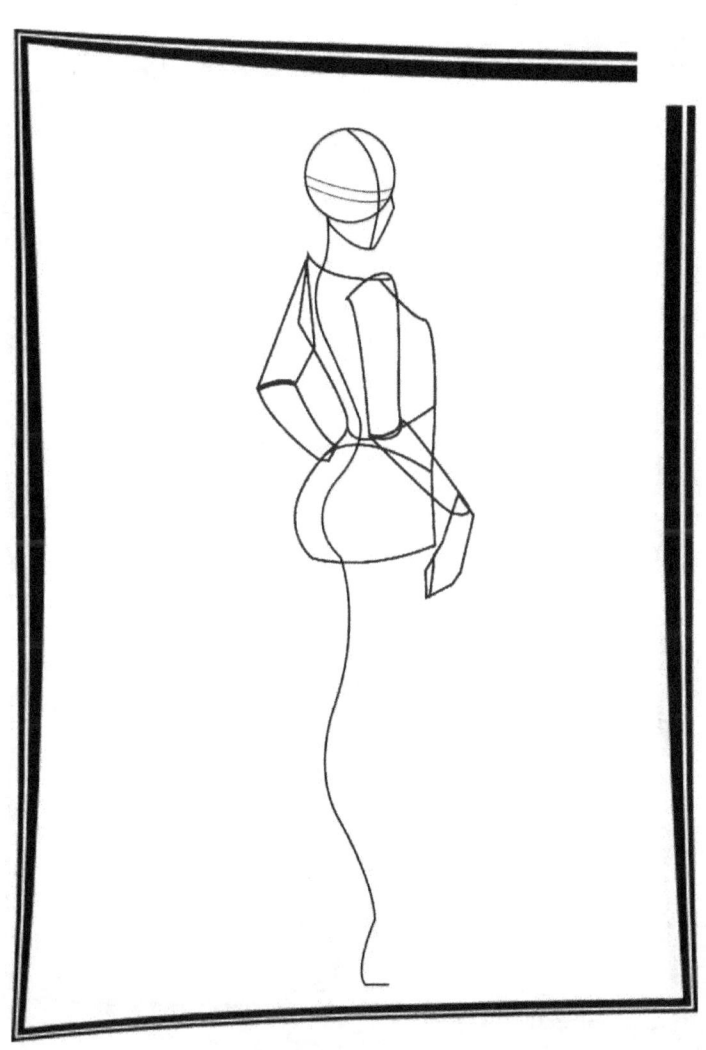

STEP 2

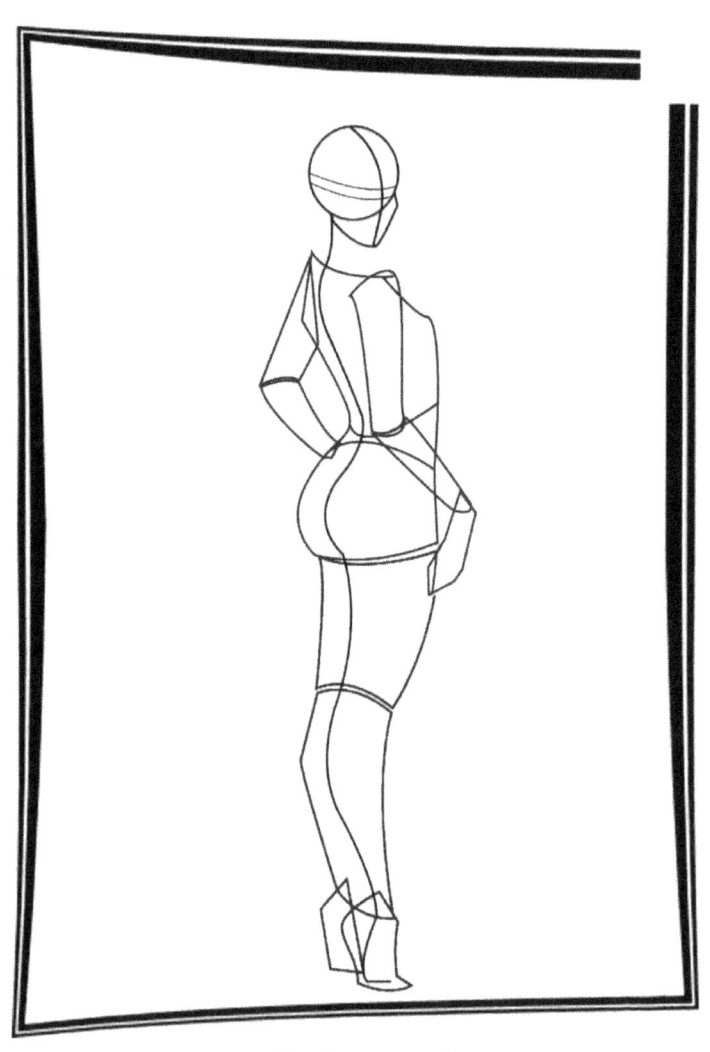

STEP 3

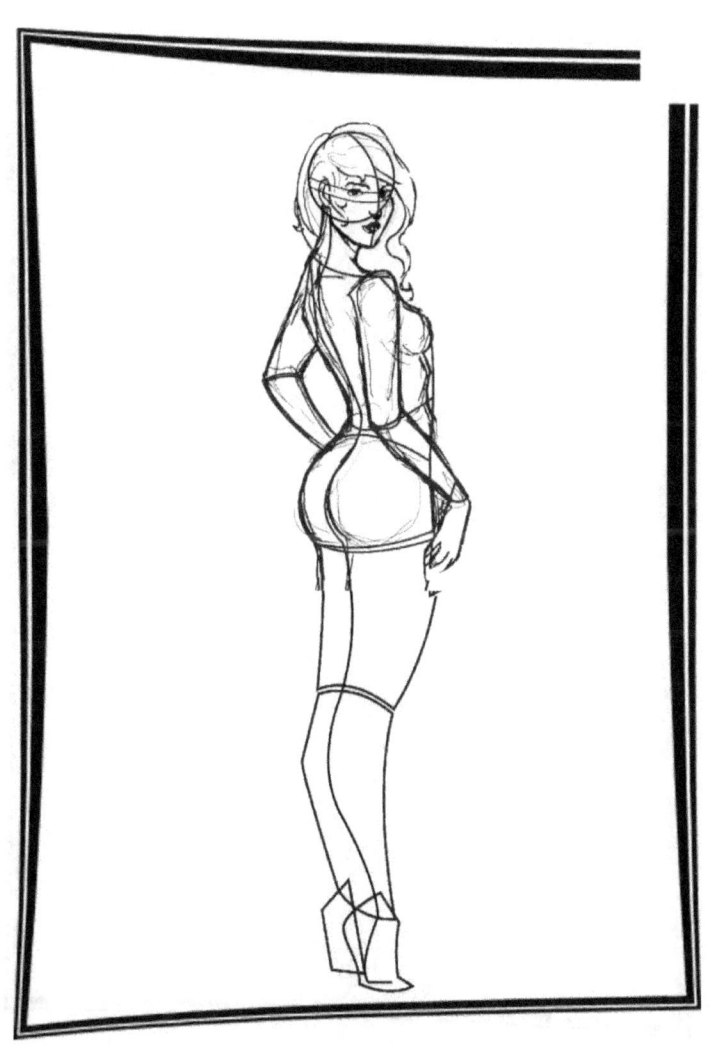

STEP 4

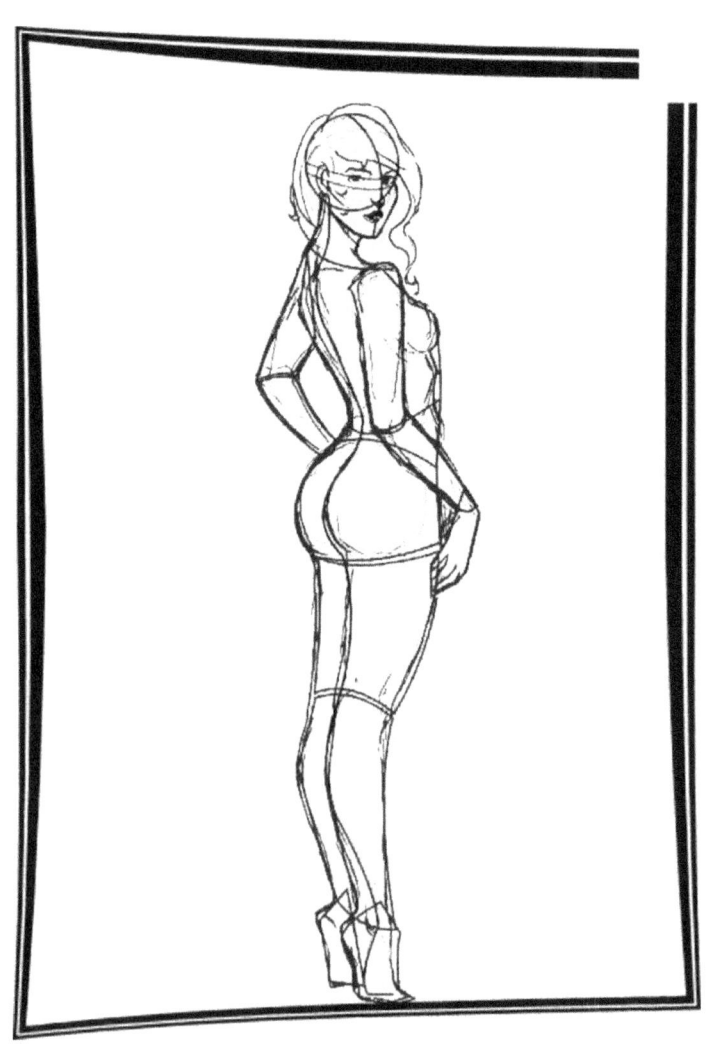

STEP 5

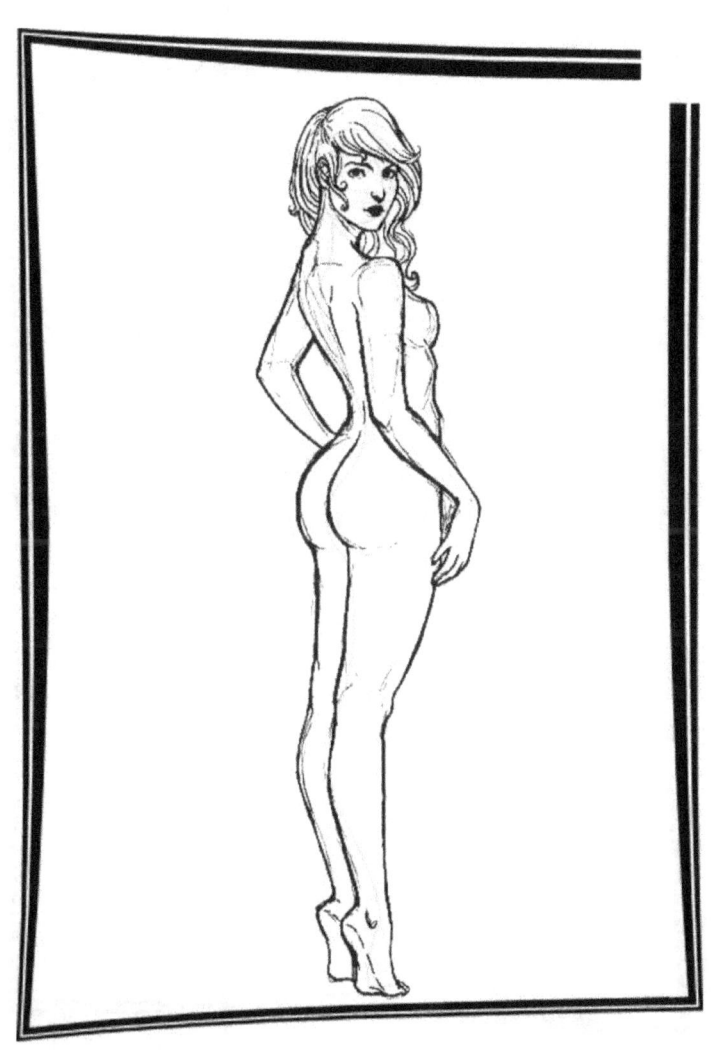

STEP 6

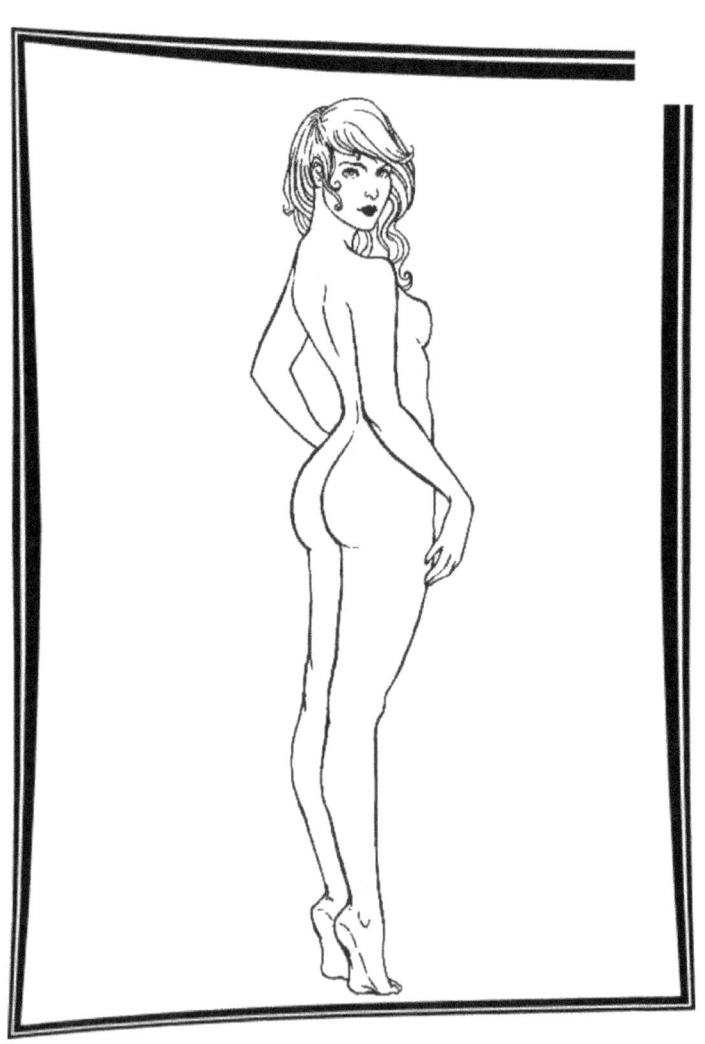

STEP 7